FLORAL DESIGN: SECOND SERIES

FLORAL DESIGN: SECOND SERIES

DOVERPICTURA

DOVER PUBLICATIONS, INC. | Mineola, New York

By Alan Weller
Designed by Juliana Trotta

Floral Design: Second Series is a new work, first published by Dover Publications, Inc., in 2011.

The CD-ROM file names correspond to the images in the book. All of the artwork stored on the CD-ROM can be imported directly into a wide range of design and word-processing programs on either Windows or Macintosh platforms. No further installation is necessary.

ISBN 13: 978-0-486-99033-0
ISBN 10: 0-486-99033-8

Manufactured in the United States of America by Courier Corporation
99033801
www.doverpublications.com

006

007

008

9

010

011

012

013

014

015

016

017

018

14

019

020

021

022

023

024

16

025

026

028

029

031

032

033

034

035

036

038

039

041

040

042

043

044

045

046

047

048

049

050

051

052

054

055

056

057

058

060

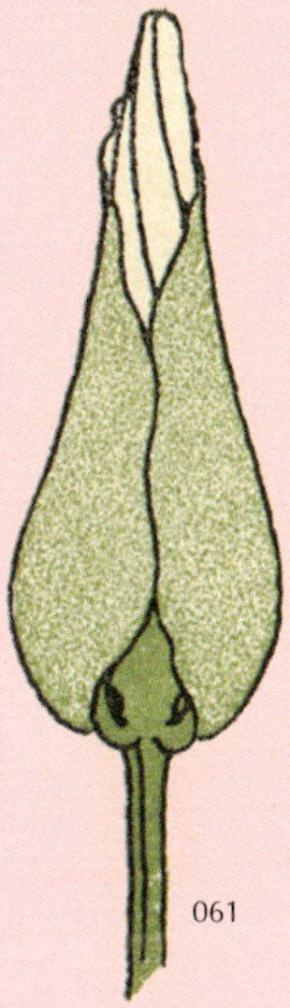

061

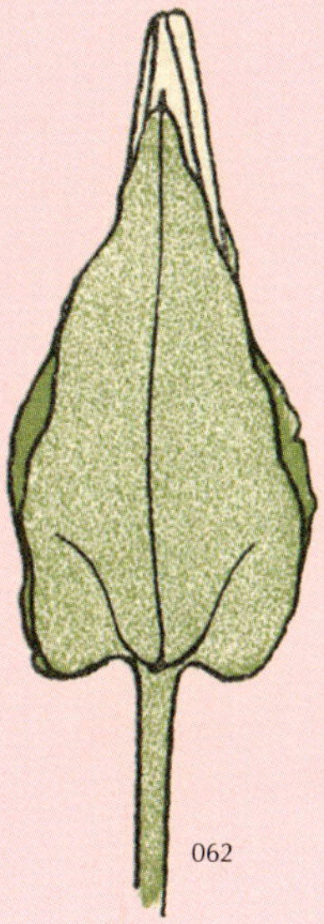

062

063

064

065

066

067

34

068

069

070

071

073

074

075

076

077

078

079

080

081

083

084

085

086

087

088

089

090

091

092

093

44

094

095

096

45

097

098

MENU

100

102

103

104

105

106

107

110

111

112

113

APRIL · 1902

FLACH ORNAMENTE

114

115

116

117

118

119

120

123

124

125

126

127

128

129 130 131

132

133

134

135

136

139

140

141

142

143

144

145

146

147

148

149

150

151

BИCHƎCHMИCK

152

153

154

155

156

157

158

159

160

161

162

163

164

165

166

167

168

169

170

171

DIVEKY.

172

173

174

175

176

177

178

179

180

181

182

183

184

185

186

189

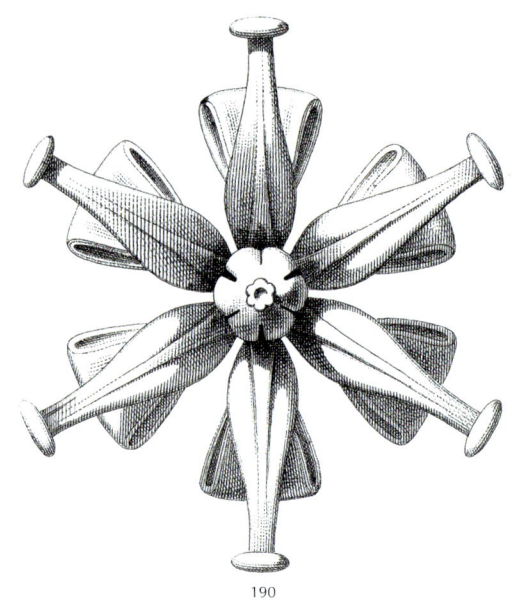

190

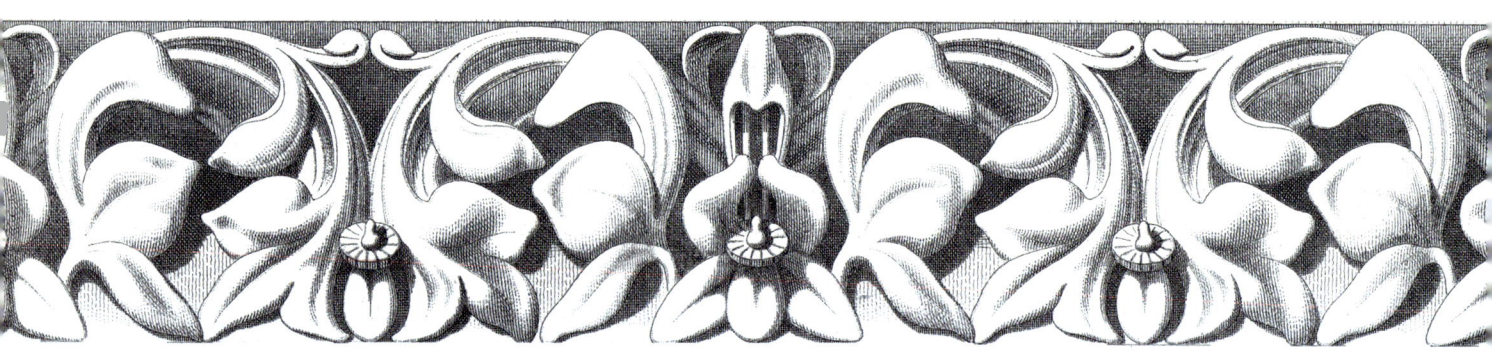

191

192

193

194

195

196

197

198

199

200

94

201

202

203

204

206

207

208

209

210

211

212

213

214

215

216

217

218

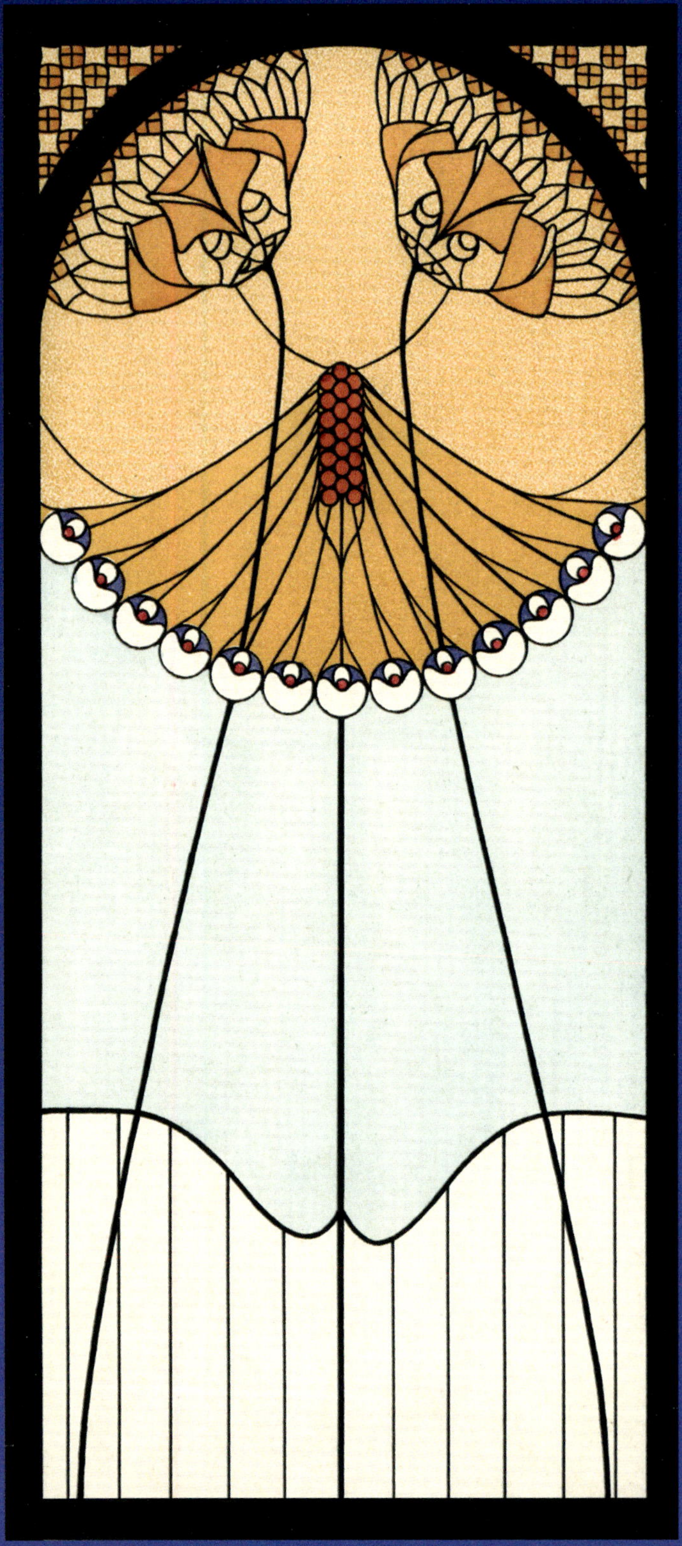

219

220

221

222

223

224

225

226

227

228

229

230

231

232

233

234

235

236

237

238   239   240   241   242

243

244

245

246

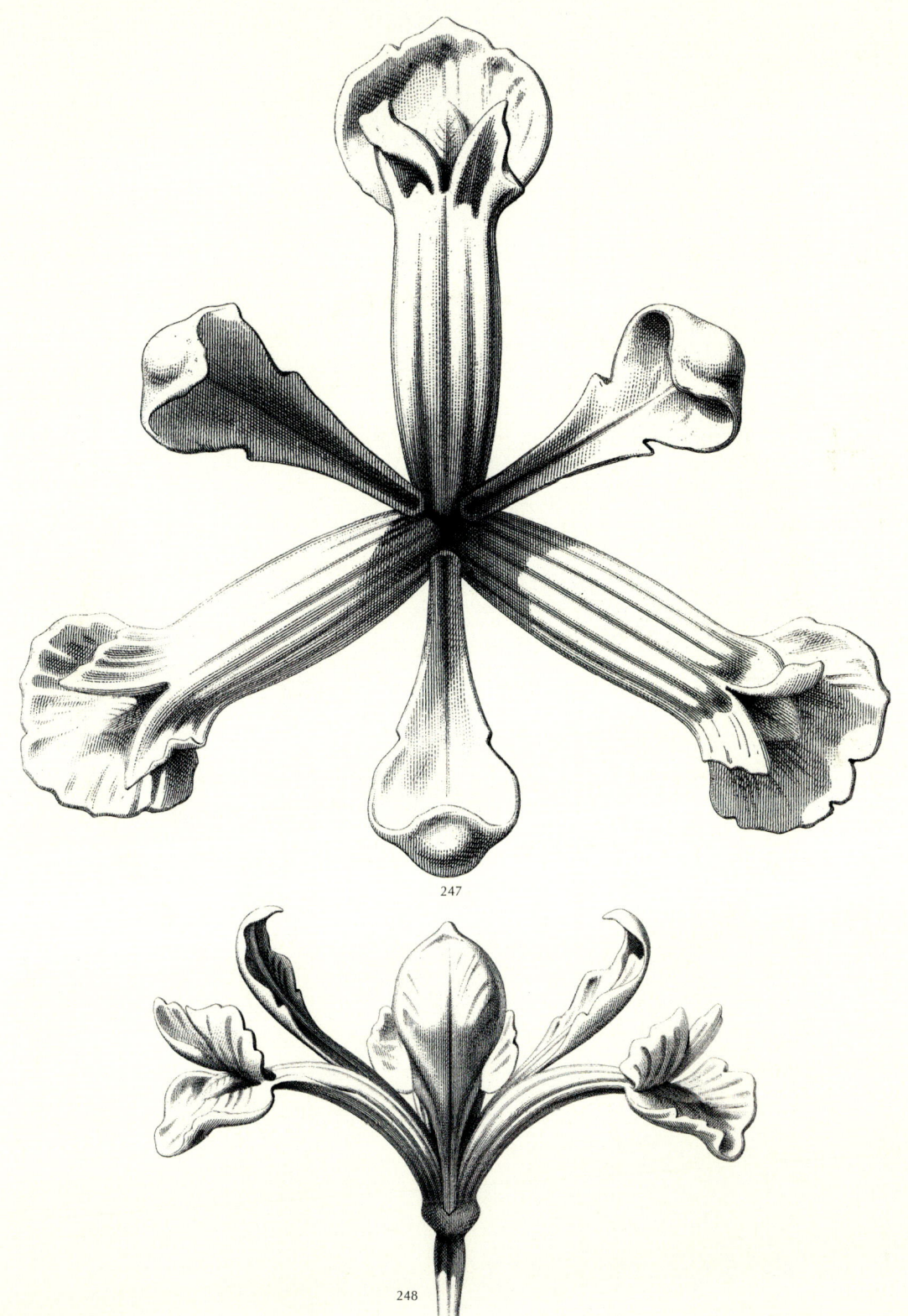

247

248

249

250

253

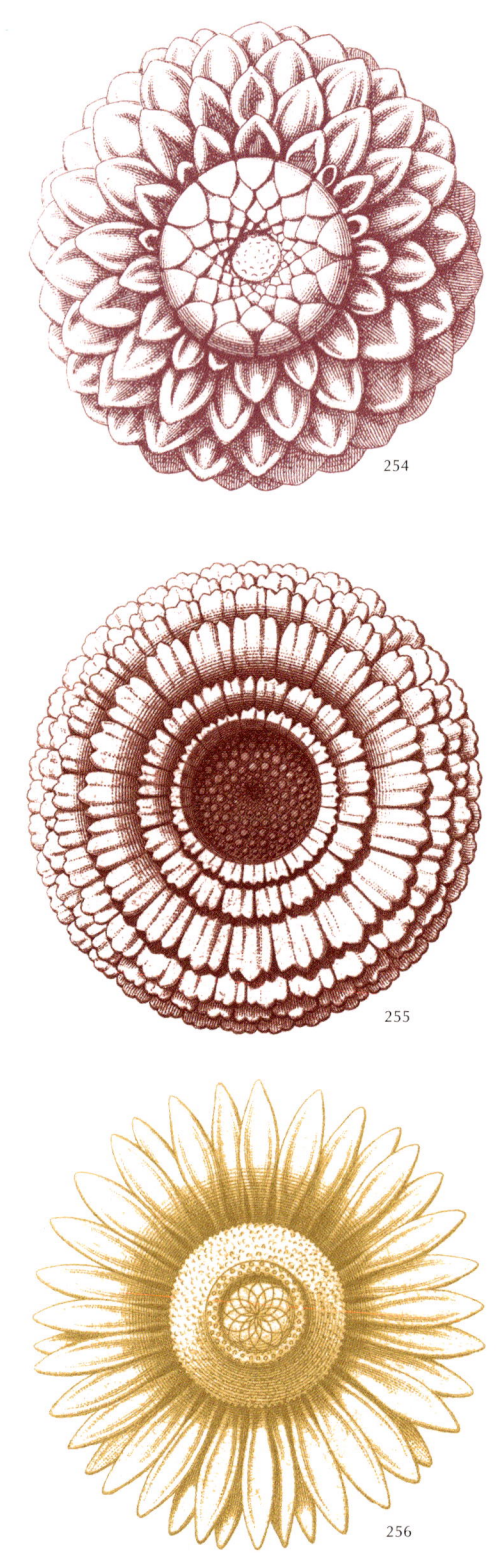

254

255

256

258